the COLL

Fig

SAGE
PRESS

SAGE PRESS

PO Box Nº 1, Rye, East Sussex TN36 6HN.
e.mail: sagepress.bm@btinternet.com
www.sagepress.co.uk

Set in Palatino italic 9 on 11 point leading.
Display in Palatino Bold Italic 14 point.

Design and Illustrations
Chris Monk of Yellowduck Design & Illustration.

Research and Text
Mrs Bobby Meyer

ISBN: 0 - 9542297 - 2 - X

Printed in England

Acknowledgements
Sage Press would like to thank Berrin Torolsan, Publishing Director of
Cornucopia magazine, for her kind permission to reproduce the text on
page 14 and both Fergus Garrett, Head Gardener at Great Dixter, Northiam,
East Sussex and Jim Buckland, Head Gardener at West Dean Gardens,
West Sussex for all their help.

Cover illlustration: see page 24

 # Fig

"Hear the voice of the fig tree:
'Compliments to my lady.
Who more noble than I?
Why not I your servant, if you have none?
They brought me from Smyrna
as plunder for the beloved'"

A moving eulogy to the glory of the fig dating back some
3,000 years or more, found on an Ancient Egyptian
papyrus. Translation by Ezra Pound & Noel Stock, from
Boris de Rachewiltz' literal renderings, into french, from the
original hieroglyphics.

The fruit of the fig tree, which we most commonly know
today in its convenient and nutritious dried form, is one of
the most ancient fruits known to civilization, dating back
5,000 years or more to the Ancient Egyptians. In biblical
writings it ranked with the grape and the olive as the most
important fruits of that time.

The Tajik Mountains of Transcaucasia are thought to have
been the original home of the wild fig tree and it was most
probably the enterprising Phoenician traders who helped
make the fig known and appreciated throughout the
Mediterranean Basin. It is believed that they also took it
with them to trade as far afield as India and China.

'Sad hillocks of archaeological mud surround it, where fig trees grow on the bare ground …'
Freya Stark describing the Temple of Artemis at Ephesus in Ionia, a Quest (1956)

Because the wild fig or caprifig is unfussy about the soil it needs, prolific in the most unpromising of locations – provided it can enjoy warmth and some humidity – and capable of producing two or even three harvests a year, it is hardly surprising that it was embraced and cultivated by so many different Mediterranean cultures through the ages.

The delicious purple-skinned fruit is wonderful eaten ripe, freshly plucked from the tree, or dried and amber-coloured for keeping during the winter months – ideal for travelling and a staple of the nomad's diet.

Not only has the fruit of the fig tree been highly prized through the ages, but also the shade afforded by its spreading branches and generous lobed foliage, under which to rest from the searing Mediterranean sun.

'They shall sit every man under his vine and under his fig tree', Micah 4:4

The disciple Nathaniel (also thought to have been known as Bartholomew) is written of in biblical texts as sitting under a fig tree and can be seen portrayed thus in the Poor Man's Bible Windows in the north aisle of Canterbury Cathedral, Kent.

Fig Varieties and their Differences

It is useful to know the subtle but important differences between the three main types of cultivated fig, which are: Common Fig, Smyrna and San Pedro. There is also the wild fig or caprifig, which is widely distributed in Turkey and without which the Smyrna would be unable to fruit.

Most species of figs found around the world are monoecious, that is, the male and female flowers are to be found in a single syconium or the multiple fruit found inside the flask-shaped inflorescence of the fig. Both the caprifig, also known as the wild goat fig, and the most commonly grown variety of fig in the United Kingdom, the Common or Brown Turkey, are self-fertilizing and do not require an outside pollinator.

Whilst both the caprifig and the Brown Turkey are self-fertile, they have a distinct and fascinating difference: the Brown Turkey produces fruits which are edible raw, whereas those of the caprifig are not. They can only be used once cooked and preserved in honey or sugar, which is a very traditional Turkish delicacy.

There is an important link, however, between the caprifig and the Smyrna. The latter is not self-fertile and relies on the fig wasp, or Blastophaga, which breeds in the caprifig, for pollination.

So the Smyrna harvest is inextricably linked with the caprifig and these orchards are always planted with a number of wild or caprifigs. This practice is almost as old as civilization and writings describing the cultivation of the

Smyrna fig and its reliance on pollination by the fig wasp date back to Aristotle and beyond.

The life-cycle of the fig wasp revolves entirely around the fig. In fact, when the Smyrna fig was first introduced as a potential commercial crop to California in the late 19th century, the growers were for years completely stumped by the trees' failure to produce fruit. Someone had overlooked the fact that the Smyrna does not produce male flowers and its need therefore for the fig wasp to act as pollinator. But even when the fig wasps were eventually brought over, they failed to overwinter and it took many years of research before this problem was overcome and by this method they could finally harvest what has become known as the Calimyrna fig.

This little wasp breeds and overwinters as larvae in galls of the fruit of the caprifig's winter crop – the first of three produced by the caprifig and known as the 'mamme' crop. In April the larvae emerges as an adult and the male impregnates the female. Soon the wingless and almost blind male dies and the winged female emerges covered in pollen, to seek out the fruit of the Smyrna. She enters it through a tiny hole known as the ostiole and completes the pollination process.

Should for some reason the pollination not take place, because the larvae have been killed by a frost for instance, then the fig farmers hang 'necklaces' of caprifigs in their Smyrna orchards and by this method the pollination process is activated.

The San Pedro fig, grown in California, is the most confounding of all: it produces two crops, with the spring fruit developing parthenocarpically, i.e. self-fertilizing, and then the second requiring caprification.

Figs for Philosophers

The ancient philosophers, Plato among them, valued the fig for its high nutritious value, claiming that it was good for both the mind and the body. Plato is thought to have eaten huge quantities and recommended it heartily to all fellow-thinkers!

Fig in the Bible

The fig has a truly ancient history with traces of seeds being found in site excavations of early settlements – some dating back almost 6,000 years.

The Bible is said to be the richest source of references to the fig, the most famous of all being in the Book of Genesis, 3:7:

'And they sewed fig leaves together and made themselves aprons. And they heard the voice of the Lord God walking in the garden in the cool of the day'.

From this time onwards perhaps dates a certain ambiguity in the very varied symbolism relating to the fig. In Hebrew, for instance, the word for the fig also has a meaning close to sexual passion or desire.

The softly plump shape of the ripened fig and the knowledge of a myriad seeds hidden within is the inspiration for one of the oldest symbols of female sexuality and fertility.

Traditions

Fig Sunday was an old country name for the Sunday before Easter, Palm Sunday. It was a tradition to eat figs on that day, to commemorate the blasting of the barren fig tree by Jesus (Mark xi).

Judas Iscariot is said to have hung himself on a fig tree.

The Romans offered the first juicy, ripe fig of the season to be plucked off the tree to the God Mercury and this led to the expression 'Mercury fig', an interesting proverbial saying which today could refer to both the earliest fruit and first artistic works.

The Romans

To the superstitious Romans – whose mythology has it that the wolf who suckled the infants Romulus and Remus rested under a fig tree – there was also a dark and evil side to this useful amd prolific tree.
In favourable growing conditions it can quickly become rampant and out of control.
It is known for producing a massive root

system and there are accounts of figs clambering over temple roofs and threatening to swamp the whole building. This was seen as a profane occurance, requiring not only the fig to be chopped down, but also the destruction of the temple itself, to be sure of delivering the sacred site from all possible evil.

However, this sinister aspect of the fig did not stop the Romans from cultivating and enjoying its harvest. Pliny tells us that he knew of no less than 29 different fig varieties growing in his native land, adding that the finest were produced in the fertile plains around Naples and in particular at Herculaneum.

This is indeed borne out by archaeological finds of dried figs almost 2,000 years later - amongst the ruins of nearby Pompeii . And there they are again, depicted in colourful wall paintings of elegant Pompeiian banquets. Pliny's writings lead us to believe that figs featured large in the diet of the slave class – their high nutritive value keeping them strong and energetic to serve their masters perhaps?

He also provides an amusing account of the watchmen whose duty it was to guard the fig orchards from thieves. Their cunning Roman masters gradually reduced their bread rations as the fruit ripened, knowing from their visibly spreading stomachs that they were gorging themselves on the rich fruits. As soon as the fruits had been picked the men are said to have slimmed down again to their old weight.

Xerxes and Attica

'I shan't buy my Attic figs in future, but grow them (myself)' – an expression rarely used today, warning that it is unwise to build castles in the air – keep your feet on the ground!

The famous Attic figs of classical Greece are traditionally thought to have been introduced from the lush and fertile region of Caria in present-day Turkey and were so prized that the warrior King of Persia, Xerxes, declared he would conquer the land of Attica for their figs. After many battles he was finally defeated by the Greeks.

The Spartans

The Spartan soldiers of Ancient Greece, known for their athletic prowess and daring courage are said to have lived almost entirely on a diet of figs! The magic fruit was thought to give them extra strength and swiftness.

Although this assertion should not be taken too literally, the fig doubtless was prominent on their daily table, as the Greeks are known to have even passed a law forbidding the best of the fig harvest to be exported.

The fig certainly is a healthy and handy source of quick energy. By drying the fruit, its exceptionally high sugar content is doubled – to 55%.

The Assyrians appreciated the sweetness and were using a syrup made from figs as a sugar substitute already some 3,000 years before Christ. It also contains important minerals such as calcium and potassium, but only a small quantity of Vitamin C, which reduces to half the value when dried.

The Ancients also discovered that it makes it an excellent ingredient for meat tenderizers or marinades and today we know that this is because the fig contains a protein-digesting enzyme.

The Fig in Turkey

*'…. the three-leaved fig which Strabo
(in Pliny's Natural History) mentions
in the valley grows there still'.*
Freya Stark, Ionia, A Quest (1956)

*'This is the kingdom of figs. The mightiest and happiest of
fig trees grow wild here everywhere, hanging over cliffs
against the sea, adorning the scattered fragments of classical
ruins in the valley, shading gardens and streets in the towns'.*
Berrin Torolsan, Cornucopia Magazine – Turkey for
Connoisseurs, Issue 16, 1998.

*Although the fig has sucessfully travelled worldwide and is
commercially produced in many warm climates as far apart
as California, Australia, North Africa and Spain, the fig
growers along the Aegean coast of Turkey continue their
historic tradition. Here half the world's crop of Smyrna figs,
around 50,000 tons, is produced – mainly for drying –
and traditionally these tempting delicacies appear on our
tables in time to herald Christmas celebrations.*

'It is pleasant to think of Themistocles in Magnesia..looking over his fields of corn and his fig trees bellying out in their straight rows, their shadows under them as if they were galleons on an arable sea'

'The great valley (of Meander) still sodden with rainwash, grew drier, warm and golden under its last crops – the cotton plants crimson, the fig-tree leaves shrivelling brown at the edges'

Freya Stark, Ionia a Quest (1956)

The Fig in England

The fig we know growing in the British Isles is the Brown Turkey or F. carica, named after the rich, fertile Caria region in Turkey. Despite our cooler climate, it is fairly common to find it as a garden tree in many of the more temperate regions of Great Britain and is thought to have originally been brought over by the Romans. It was later re-introduced from the East, possibly as early as the 12th century.

Undoubtedly the Romans brought with them dried figs in their supplies from home, as archaeological excavations around Britain can testify. Perhaps they even tried to grow them in the southern part of England, as they did grapevines. A fig tree in the protected atrium area of a rich official's house would have made sense. They certainly would have wanted to make the special Roman dish of ham boiled in a mixture of water and dried figs or even to produce the exquisitely-flavoured liver from pigs fed on dried figs before slaughter.

It was very probably Queen Eleanor, a former princess of Castille, who would have insisted on including some figs on a Spanish shipment of oranges and lemons which arrived at Portsmouth in 1289. And by the end of the 14th century the enterprising Spanish and Italian spice traders were bringing raisins of Corinth, figs and dates into England for consumption in vast quantities by those wealthy citizens who could afford such luxuries. For the poor, figs were restricted to Christmas, fasting days and Lent and were used for festive pottages and pies.

One such pottage was known as 'figgey' - bread and figs boiled in highly-spiced wine, raisins and pine nuts – and commonly made for eating during Lent.

Given a warm, sheltered environment, colonies of wild-growing figs are to be found overhanging sheltered railway embankments, car parks (benefitting from the warmth of exhaust fumes) canals and even growing out of a grave, which Richard Mabey in The Concise Edition of Flora

Britannica *suggests might result from a snack taken by the occupant before dying. Mabey goes on to recount a local legend that this tree sprang from the grave of an atheist, who had the foresight to ask for a fig to be put in the coffin, saying that if there was life beyond the grave then the fig would sprout!*

The reason for figs flourishing on canalside sites may well have a lot to do with the felicitous combination of the unusually warm water temperature, heated up from factory outfalls, and passing barges carrying dried goods such as raisins, figs etc. Picnic remnants could also account for seed-sowing.

'Train up a fig tree in the way it should go, and when you are old sit under the shade of it'
Captain Cuttle
in Dombey & Son *by Charles Dickens.*

Figs in London

The adaptability of the fig is extraordinary – in the early 18th century, the nurseryman and pioneer hybridiser, Thomas Fairchild enjoyed walking through the City of London observing plants and trees and in his diaries made particular note of two fig trees which were surviving and producing fruit in seemingly difficult conditions:

' … although encompassed with houses on every side which are so high that the sun never reaches them in winter'.

Fairchild muses on the possibility of the so-adaptable fig being planted more widely in city gardens and produce luscious fruit for its owners.

In his diaries Fairchild notes how he passes on advice to the parish priest at St. Giles Church, Cripplegate on a new way of pruning fig trees, although maddeningly there are no more details of this new method.
The Ingenious Mr. Fairchild
by Michael Leapman

Louis XIV and a love of figs

This luscious and sensuous fruit was one of the Sun King's favourites. He grew a number of different varieties at the Palace of Versailles – very possibly in his Orangerie, which would have been ideal – one of which was named La Versaillaise, later renamed 'Royale' in his honour.

In the 19th century demand in the French capital for exotic fruit was so great that huge orchards growing peaches, apricots and figs were successfully established outside Paris. Extensive fig plantations were centred around the Argenteuil area – one variety grown was known as the 'Blanche d'Argenteuil'.

The fig trees flourished and fruited well, provided the trees were protected from the frosts and this was done in a very clever way. They were planted at an angle, overhanging a shallow trench. Come winter, they were pruned very hard, leaving only the most supple branches and then carefully bound with ropes and covered with a thick layer of straw and dead leaves. Today, growers North of the Loire still have to protect their fig trees, but they leave them upright, tying the tree together and wrapping it up in layers of plastic bubblewrap, with a covering of dried straw and the top left open sufficiently to allow air to circulate and avoid the tree getting mouldy.

Figs under Glass

Together with pineapples, bananas and other exotics, figs have been grown in England for hundreds of years by the wealthy in their own hothouses. It was still common to do so until the early part of the 20th century. Figs grow so vigorously that they can soon take over if not kept in check by judicious pruning. But even today, where hothouses are still maintained or have been renovated, it remains an alternative to siting them outdoors against a sunny and protected wall – often in a walled kitchen garden.
Apart from the obvious protection from inclement weather a distinct advantage of growing under glass is that the number of harvests per year can be increased.

Jim Buckland, Head Gardener at West Dean Gardens, near Chichester West Sussex, tells how the estate's two magnificent centenarian Brown Turkey figs, which ripen to a dark plum colour, can be managed to produce two and even three crops a year. Each is growing in separate hothouses: in the cool lower house, the fig produces two harvests and in the top house which is heated in the winter months, the number of crops increases to three. A guide to picking the fruit: it is at its best is when a droplet of a sugary secretion appears at the small opening known as the ostiole. Wait too long and the fruit will split.

In the mid-19th century the seaside town of Worthing, West Sussex, was well known for its market gardens where, along with the tomatoes and cucumbers, grapes and figs were also grown under glass commercially – an industry which was still thriving in the late 1940's.

The history of growing figs in Worthing dates back to a much earlier time however. There is a tradition that the first fig tree was brought over from Normandy in the 12th century and planted not far from Worthing, at Sompting. Another story recounts how Thomas Becket planted a fig tree in West Tarring (today part of Worthing), at the Palace of the Archbishop of Canterbury.

Worthing Fig Gardens

Today it is impossible to untangle legend from history, but the fact remains that West Tarring is indeed known for its figs. Exploring the winding streets of this charming area a number of fig trees can still be spotted in the gardens of old houses and outside one, known as Bishops Garth, there is an intriguing plaque marking the site of the Ancient Fig Garden.

According to a letter written by a Mr. Edward Sayers to the local Worthing Gazette in 1905, the Fig Garden was planted in 1745 by his great-great-grandfather, John Long, using old stock from the nearby Rectory Garden. So this was indeed continuing a well-established old tradition.

The Fig Garden or orchard was laid out in walks and a popular tourist attraction, where in the summer cream teas where served to visitors. It is said that Edward Lear visited them in 1858 to make sketches for a painting he was planning and there are accounts of how locals would walk over the fields from Worthing to enjoy the tea and – when ripe - all the figs they could eat! The gardens are known to have still been open right up to 1936, but were closed after the war and the house is now a private home. Sadly, many of the trees were lost when some of the garden was sold for redevelopment.

And another legend - this time for bird-watchers to enjoy: A small fig-eating bird of the warbler family, known as the beccafico, is said to have migrated every summer from Italy to West Tarring for a week only, to feast on the figs.

This little bird is also said to have been spotted at Sompting where there too are a number of very ancient fig trees. Although a romantic tale, there is sadly little evidence to back it up.

Cultivation

The fig lends itself to training up a sunny wall in a fan shape or – given the time, skill and patience – in an endless series of curls, as at Pashley Manor, East Sussex.

The Victorian gardeners came up with some very original ideas, such as a 'figwam' still to be seen today in the beautiful gardens of Quex House, Birchington, Kent. A number of Brown Turkey figs have been trained over a dome structure to create a shelter for lawnmowers when it rained.

Needless to say, the story has it that the gardeners then had to walk quite a way to find shelter themselves in a garden hut!

Nutritional value

Although the fruit of the fig only contains a small amount of Vitamin C, 2mg/100g when fresh, it does have a high potassium content, 200 mg/100g and is rich in glucose and fructose sugars. In fact, Pliny the Roman writer comments on how fat the guards in the fig plantations become as the season progresses and that they slim down again during the winter.

The drying process of the fruit not only serves to preserve them over the winter months, but also increases their sugar and potassium value almost five-fold. Curiously, the Vitamin C content, however, is halved. Although there does not appear to be any firm scientific data, it is said that dried figs also contain other vital life-enhancing ingredients.

Figs are used in some bakery products and when dried can be roasted and added to coffee to produce what is known as 'Viennese coffee'.

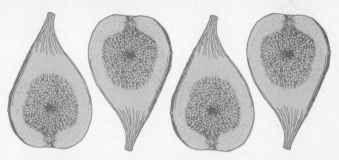

Recipes for Desserts

Compote of Figs
Dried figs soaked overnight in sufficient red or white wine
to cover and then cooked slowly with spices such as cloves
and cinammon, to which is added thin slices of lemon, make
a fragrant and delicious dessert served hot or cold, either on
its own or with double cream.

Stuffed figs
A Turkish recipe still used today dates back to the Roman
predeliction for stuffing dried figs: First soak them overnight
in water or simply boil them briefly until they plump up.
Cut off the stalk tops and stuff with walnut halves. Fill the
base of a wide pan with the stuffed fruit and pour over a cup
of milk. Simmer gently until liquid has all but disappeared.
This is excellent either hot or cold and is even better served
with cream.

The Romans are said to have enjoyed a simpler method,
preserving the soaked, stuffed figs in honey rather than
cooking them.

Figs can be crystallised and a
traditional Turkish recipe uses small
unripe figs, sugar and the juice of a lemon. Homemade jam,
using freshly-picked figs is quite unusual and produces a
very fragrant, beautiful pink-coloured translucent confection.
Many Moorish-inspired recipes for sweetmeats can be found
in the Algarve, Portugal, using dried figs ground to a paste
with nuts. And we ourselves carry on this tradition in some
of our biscuits, such as fig rolls.

Savoury figs
The subtle sweet flavour of fresh figs can be successfully
blended with that of the stronger more pungent anchovy:

Corsican Anchoiade with figs
Soak 5 anchovy fillets to remove salt and wipe dry. Pound
them with 1 lb. (500g) fresh figs and a small garlic clove.
Spread paste on slices of bread moistened with olive oil.
Sprinkle with chopped onions and serve as an hors d'oeuvre.

Medicinal Uses

Figs act as a demulcent and are used in preparations for treatment of catarrh in the nose and throat. Because of the high fibre content it is also a mild laxative when taken as a syrup.

If roasted and then split, the soft pulp inside the fruit can be used as a poultice for gumboils and dental abcesses.

The milky juice oozing from the freshly broken stalk of the fig has been used for removing warts or to dry them up.

Figs are so plentiful in Southern Spain, that it is common for the local farmers to feed them to their lucky and undoubtedly contented pigs!

The Romans dedicated the fig to the god Bacchus.

Although there is no hard historical or written evidence to back up the story, legend has it that Livia tried repeatedly to kill her husband, the Roman Emperor Augustus.

However, suspecting Livia of such infamous behaviour, Augustus refused to eat anything except fruits which he himself had picked. Nothing daunted, the story has it that the cunning Livia actually smeared poison on the figs as they hung on the tree.

Robert Graves immortalises the imaginary scenario in I, Claudius, *when he has Livia say to her son Tiberius 'By the way, don't eat the figs...'*

'I saw my life branching out before me like
the green fig tree in the story. From the top
of every branch, like a fat purple fig,
a wonderful future beckoned and winked.
One fig was a husband and a happy
home.'
'The Bell Jar' by Sylvia Plath

A contemporary 20th century quotation,
picturing the fig tree as a complex map of
life's journey, with its many choices
symbolized by the luscious and tempting
fruit, waiting to be plucked along the way.

Botanical Notes

Common Name:
Brown Turkey Fig,
edible Fig, common Fig.

Botanical Name:
Ficus carica L. (after the
region of Caria in Turkey).

Family:
Moraceae, as also mulberry
and pomegranate.

Wood:
Not used today, but some
Ancient Egyptian coffins
made of fig wood have been
found.

Size:
Grows as a large rambling
shrub which responds well
to hard pruning. Can reach
2 – 5m tall, even up to 10m.
If grown near a house wall,
best to contain roots in a
sunken pot.

Branches:
Can be trained against
a wall and tied into a fan
or spirals. Regular pruning
to cut out any frosted or
damaged branches and old
wood, results in
better fruiting
performance.

Fruit:

The F. carica is self-fertile and produces globular-shaped fruits. Ribbed, textured grey-green outer skin, which is peeled to reveal fleshy purple-red interior with numerous seeds. Exudes a milky latex when fresh, which can cause skin problems around the mouth. Does not travel well, so bulk of the harvest is preserved by drying before shipping.

Leaves:

Large palmate, dark green and rather fleshy, with 3-5 deep lobes. Chopped up finely can be used as a substitute for mulberry leaves to feed silkworms.

Propagation:

The Fig is deciduous.
Not difficult to propogate from cuttings taken in spring or summer or by layering.

Bark:

Grey, smooth.

Cultivation

Although it can be a wild and untamed tree, surviving in locations as widely different as hot, craggy Turkish cliffs and exhaust-filled British car parks, it is easy to cultivate, even on fairly indifferent soil conditions, providing it is grown in a warm, sheltered position and it is not left to dry out completely. These will over-winter successfully and produce ripe fruits the following year.

Once the risk of frost is over, another bout of thinning is advantageous, to remove both old wood and any wood near the tips that has been caught by the frost. What is left should also be cut back fairly hard to encourage new growth from near the main stem.

Care should be taken to leave all good shoots carrying the small as yet unripe fruits.

Opinions vary, but it is thought that the genus Ficus contains around some 1,000 species, widely-distributed throughout all the warmer climates around the world. This includes the Indian rubber plant (F. elastica) and the extraordinary Indian banyan or weeping (F. benghalensis) – commonly called the 'strangler fig' because of the way it produces aerial roots and eventually kills the host tree.

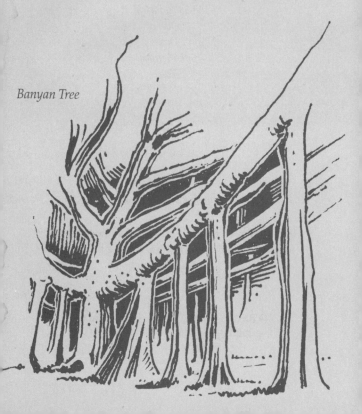

Banyan Tree

In the same series

Ash
Box
Caring for Box
Cedar of Lebanon
Hawthorn
Holly
Monkey Puzzle
Mulberry
Oak
Sitka Spruce
Yew

Also available

The Puzzle Puzzle Jigsaw

Future Titles

Black Poplar
Wild Service Tree
Willow for Basketmakers

If you enjoyed this title and would like to buy any
of the above titles or require further information
please contact

SAGE PRESS
PO Box Nº 1, Rye, East Sussex TN36 6HN.
e-mail: sagepress.bm@btinternet.com
www.sagepress.co.uk